RED MANGO

OTHER PLAYS BY CHARLES TIDLER:

Blind Dancers
Straight Ahead
The Farewell Heart
I Could Sleep for a Thousand Years
The Butcher's Apron
Fabulous Yellow Roman Candle
The Sex Change Artist
The Art of Kindness
Café Voyeur

RED MANGO

a blues

by Charles Tidler

ANVIL PRESS • VANCOUVER

Red Mango

Copyright © 2001 by Charles Tidler

All rights reserved. No part of this book may be reproduced by any means without the prior written permission of the publisher, with the exception of brief passages in reviews. Any request for photocopying or other reprographic copying of any part of this book must be directed in writing to the Canadian Copyright Licensing Agency (CANCOPY) One Yonge Street, Suite 1900, Toronto, Ontario, Canada, M5E 1E5.

Permission to perform or give readings of this play, whether by amateurs or professionals, must be obtained in advance from the author: Charles Tidler, c/o The Belfry Theatre, 1291 Gladstone Avenue, Victoria, B.C. V8T 1G5

The publisher gratefully acknowledges the financial assistance of the B.C. Arts Council, the Canada Council for the Arts, and the Book Publishing Industry Development Program (BPIDP) for their support of our publishing program.

The playwright gratefully acknowledges the support and kindness of the B.C. Arts Council, the Playwrights Theatre Centre, and the Belfry Theatre, particularly the love and support of Roy and Mary, during the development of this script.

Printed and bound in Canada
Cover design: Rayola Graphic Design
Author photo: Frances Litman

CANADIAN CATALOGUING IN PUBLICATION DATA

Tidler, Charles.
Red mango

(Anvil Performance Series, ISSN 1188-0872; no. 4)
A play.
ISBN: 1-895636-38-8 : 11.95

I. Title
PS3570.I27R4 2001   812'.54   C00-911574-9

Represented in Canada by the Literary Press Group
Distributed by General Distribution Services

Anvil Press
Suite 204-A 175 East Broadway,
Vancouver, B.C. V5T 1W2 CANADA
www.anvilpress.com

Red Mango is a blues dialogue for a male actor and a guitarist.

CHARACTER:
CHARLIE, late 40s.

PLACE:
Bars, clubs and coffeehouses of Victoria, B.C.

TIME:
Winter & Spring.

The design is minimalist. A table and two chairs. Some room to dance. A scrim and a small stage for the blues guitarist.

Red Mango premiered at Victoria's Belfry Theatre in April 2000, with the following cast:

> CHARLIE . . . . Michael Hogan
> GUITARIST . . . . Harris Van Berkel

Directed by John Cooper. Set and costume design by Carole Klemm. Lighting design by Ian Rye. The stage manager was Lisa Cochran.

Director's Notes:

THE BLUES IS Black folk music that grew out of the post-slavery African-American experience. Its sources lie in the fields and juke joints filled with black workers and the Black churches of the southern United States. The songs spin tales of hardship and survival, good times and bad times, suffering and celebration, and ultimately an indomitable spirit. Its peak popularity as a form spans the period from the 1920s to the 1950s. Blues is generally seen as a Black American music.

Yet, today, every Canadian city has at least one or two blues clubs, some have several, and you would find them full mostly of non-black Canadians playing to audiences mostly comprised of other non-black Canadians, the majority of whom are free from the horrific types of social and economic oppression experienced by the American blacks of the first half of the 20th century. And still, the blues is played and drunk in with true passsion and I suspect true recognition. Why is this? Why such popularity? Why such affinity? With so many Canadians worshipping and testifying at the church of the blues, we must be responding to something special in this music. Perhaps it is the passion, perhaps it is the joy. Perhaps some universal truths are celebrated in this form. What is our relationship to this form from another time and place? What does our enthusiastic embracing of the form say about us? Are there now Canadian blues stories to be told? I think *Red Mango* is a Canadian blues story which sheds some illumination on these questions.

In the blues, there is always a tension between light and dark, suffering and transcendence, the holy and the profane, the celebration and the lament. There is a kind of uplift in the naming of the woes. There is a hint of god in the devil's music. The impulse has a double edge. As a theatre director I am involved in telling stories about human beings, and therefore I am always interested in paradox and the tensions of contradiction, which I hold to be at the core of the human experience. The marriage of the blues and the theatre seems natural.

Red Mango is Charlie's blues song, a diary of his struggle through his woes and his ecstasies. It is his cry and his shout of joy. Drama, like the blues, is characterized by the tension, or conflict, arising from contradiction. Such is true of *Red Mango*. It is, after all, the diary of a celibate sensualist, flip-flopping between states of desire and reluctance, as well as despair and ecstasy, excitement and sloth, courage and fear, purposelessness and meaning. Charlie is both part of something and totally alone. Both the drama and the comedy arise from his attempts to resolve seemingly contradictory polarities which ultimately can only be balanced.

Red Mango is more a performance piece than a well-made play. Though there is a sense of linear time to the way the individual stories accumulate, the material is organized more closely in accordance with the principles of poetry than drama. Each story unfolds upon the other, a series of supercharged words, classic blues images, and richly evocative guitar licks; each story unfolding with its own rhythm, melody, attitude and raw emotion, laid out like a series of sensory polaroids shaped to the logic of a poem. There is no fourth wall and Charlie lays his life right in our laps. It is full frontal and there is no safety, no illusion of just observing. We are definitely part of the trip. We are as much in awe of the power and skill of the performances as we are seduced by the beautiful torture of a blues longing. Tools of the theatre enhance the poetry; rain drips down a window via the magic of video projection. Guitar player shifts from posture to posture, locale to locale upon a backdrop of abstracted, metal fire escapes. Moods, locales and times of day bleed effortlessly one into another under the organization of expressionistic lighting. Blues mythology and inner emotional states are revealed through slide projection, and allowed to resonate against the action. All this with a sumptuous score of the many moods and voices of the blues, conjured with passion and skill by a consummate blues guitarist. The result is more theatre poem than traditional well-made play.

And then there are the intangibles best left unexplained. Solo guitar mirroring solo human. The cumulative value of a cast of unseen colourful characters living with one foot in Charlie's blues world, the other in the imagination of each audience member. The inherent power and associative value of the music itself. The blues tradition of call/response reshaped in interplay of actor and audience. And, lest we forget, LOVE. Love of words, love of performance, love of recognition, love of sharing, and, always, love of the blues.

— *John Cooper, March 2001*

THE SET LIST:

Everything Exaggerated Is Trivial / 1

To Not Be Alone / 3

Red Wine Before Noon / 5

A Place in the Bar / 8

A Strong Stink on My Fingers / 10

The Back Door Man / 21

Four or Five Pints of Beer / 23

Raining Outside / 27

If I Done Somebody Wrong / 31

Almost Stayed Home Blues / 33

Sex in The 90s / 37

Cup of Coffee Blues / 42

The Thing To Do / 46

Here Am I / 53

The Saxophone Case / 59

This book is for
Sam
and for
Hogan

Yes.

Everything Exaggerated Is Trivial

"EVERYTHING EXAGGERATED IS TRIVIAL." Albert Camus said that. I know it sounds like something Andy Warhol said, but it was Albert Camus. "Everything exaggerated is trivial."

B.B. King advises that you should never be too proud to beg. I'm not so sure about that one, but I call my ex-lover and beg her to come back home to me.

I say I cried because I could smell you in our bed when I was the only one there.

She says I've had sex.

I say that's okay.

She says without protection.

To Not Be Alone

TO NOT BE ALONE I buy a cup of coffee, sitting here in a small café. I'm following my cock a lot. I feel like a donkey propelled forward in pursuit of a large carrot between my legs. Sex and women interest me a lot. Ass and tits and curves, sure, but I also get excited watching a woman cross the street, or stopping for a moment to fuss with a child. Women with small children turn me on. I get off just watching them in action.

I'm horny and very keen every time I get a smell of a woman. Whiff, smell, ache. A lot of women are interested in my smell, too, a lot of different kinds of women go out of their way to get close to me, and each one is a whiff of a smell that makes me ache.

I follow my carroty desires all over town. Even at home, when I answer the phone and it's a woman's voice talking this and that . . . later, after we hang up, I get down on all fours and howl like a dog.

I follow the blues scene, Saturday afternoon jam, hanging around a crowded smoky bar, drinking beer, listening to down and dirty amplified blues, looking and talking and laughing with all the women. It's a friendly, good-looking crowd of people, and there's always a lot of good, friendly sexual fun that goes with the blues, and room, too, for a sad loneliness that gets recognized in everyone.

Whiff of hair and soft bump of body, we're all alone and all together on the dance floor, jumping up and down.

Women spin, and there's no doubt that certain women, very specific and particular women, spin towards me. Bipolar magnets are cock and cunt. Some attractions are weak, and some are strong, and the strong always come right over. I always get a chance to make a strong move, aggressive, friendly, honest and cool.

When I go out to the laundromat and stop in at a café for a quick bowl of soup, the waitress winks at me and dotes. A man in a hurry turns her on.

I say I'll be back when I can stay longer.

I rush out the door to change my clothes from the washer to the dryer.

Red Wine Before Noon

SMOKING DOPE AND DRINKING red wine before noon, but a few questions nonetheless: Who am I? What am I up to? What do I hope to do with the rest of my life? I don't want to deal with any of this, and a little later I find myself dropping in on Brenda, pretty woman, who I met folding clothes at the laundromat.

Brenda is building shelves. I watch her drill some holes and drive some screws. Then, she makes tea and sandwiches. We sit on her front porch, looking down at the beach, nothing but sky and water. We don't say very much, but we tease each other a little bit about sex. Brenda suddenly grunts and takes my hand in her hand and squeezes. The sweet moment passes. Brenda says she wants to get back to work on her shelves. We hug and kiss, and I go.

Lonely day ache as palpable as the leather jacket on my back, I wander in mind and body all the way down Dallas Road, following the winter sun, the flashing water, stumbling over rock and cloud. I drift with the wind, making my way back downtown for a coffee in a café. Maybe it's the dope or maybe the wine or maybe both, but the brick wall that runs along the side of my booth appears to collide with the base of my nose. I go down below the table and pretend for a long time to be tying my shoelace.

I buy a big bottle of Greek red wine, a tub of pasta salad and a barbecue chicken. At home, I feast alone.

I think about all the beautiful women who have been kind to me today. The woman with the child on the steps of the synagogue said she was happy to see me. The woman with too many children in her apartment kissed me twice on the cheek. The nicest and prettiest woman in town was my waitress in the café. The young and beautiful playwright chatted with me perfume close while paying her bill. And a very particular woman said hello.

Brenda drops by with her friend Marie. I thought Brenda and I were going to spend an evening alone together watching a video, but no. Brenda changed the plans at the last moment and brought a friend along. The three of us have a pretty good time talking about this and that. Marie knows the dancer I think about when I masturbate. We drink from a big bottle of Jim Beam that Marie pulls out of her gym bag. We watch the video, the three of us under a blanket on the little hide-a-bed couch like three peas in a pod. We all fall fast asleep sitting up. Then, the light is on. Brenda and Marie are putting on their coats, saying good night. Goodbye, good night. And I'm left with the smells of two women in the hide-a-bed if I get down close and sniff the cushions.

The next morning I ride the bicycle to the bagel shop. I like to get there early when the bagels are hot. I always ask for hot ones, and the happy young woman behind the counter laughs and winks at me.

A Place in the Bar

I WALK OVER the causeway to James Bay and the JBI Saturday afternoon blues jam. The bar is crowded as usual, nowhere really to sit down, when bass guitarist Ernest Humingway waves me over to a standup table.

And so I have a place in the bar. I look around. Who's here today? Somebody slaps me on the butt, and I turn to the friendly smile of Willamena Passetti. She wrote her name on a napkin last week. Today, she drops a glass of dark beer in front of me. Delicious. Willamena laughs at my tip and bumps against me hip to hip, slap, and disappears with her tray of fresh beer. This is fun.

> *". . . Baby, please don't go back to*
> *New Orleans*
> *Because I love you so . . ."*

The amplified jammers wail, wringing their ragged hearts out on the little stage. I'm drinking dark beer by the glass, and every time Willamena passes by, it's hip to hip with a slap. Once it's a double slap-slap, and that's the best one. There's no way it could be by mistake.

I can't stop smiling, and in walk Brenda and Marie, two pretty women, and they say hello, you're smiling, and I say, well, you're smiling, too, and the three of us laugh.

We go outside to smoke a joint. Brenda talks me into going downtown, but it's raining hard, and we huddle together beneath an awning. Brenda says let's go, and we plunge into the downpour, all the way to Steamer's where Bill Johnston is playing with his blues trio.

> *". . . You can have all them Texas women,*
> *Save the Oklahoma girls for me . . ."*

Brenda goes off to the women's can, and a yellow crayon blonde in tight pink pants and white cowboy boots squeezes up beside me, leaning close, so close her lips lick the hairs in my right ear, telling me how in love she is with the new guitar Bill Johnston bought in Seattle last week.

The band rocks. Everybody in the bar jumps spontaneously to their feet, and we all dance, jumping, rocking, smiling and laughing. The crayon blonde presses against me, and my shirt is soaked with rain and fresh female sweat. Brenda is smiling and dancing with some guy in front of the women's can. She waves, and I wave, and the music never stops.

A Strong Stink on My Fingers

A TUESDAY AFTERNOON, I'm walking downtown in wind and rain, and run into Brenda, pretty woman, who's on the street talking to her daughter Jennifer, and Jennifer's friend a shy street kid with stringy blonde beard and a blue backpack. Jennifer wants to keep her new puppy at Brenda's place. Brenda says that's okay, but it has to stay in the bathroom. Jennifer and shy-beard wander away, and I follow Brenda into Scotts to have a coffee.

We sit back by the kitchen. Brenda knows the waitress by her first name. We drink coffee, and Brenda smokes. She was a teacher for 20 years, but now she's broke and washing dishes. What's important to her is that she hasn't had a drink in over seven years. Booze doesn't bother her at all, even hanging around in the blues bars. She asks me what I'm up to.

I say I don't know. I just hang around, talking to women every chance I get.

Brenda likes the blues scene because everybody has a really bizarre history: bikers, writers, you name it.

I like to waste time with any woman who wants to sit and waste time. I love to talk to women, but the afternoon becomes evening, and I'm sitting at home alone again. I can't stop thinking about women. I call Abe and tell him he should meet me down at Bart's for the blues jam.

Abe says I was going down to Hermann's for the blues jam there.

I say yeah, I'm going down there, too, but they're giving away free beer at Bart's.

Abe says I don't know.

Free beer, man.

Abe says is there going to be any women down there?

The place will be jumping with beautiful women guaranteed.

Abe says I don't know.

Are you alright?

Abe says I was just thinking of a quiet night for a change.

Well, I want to check out Bart's.

Abe says later.

And he's a dial tone.

> "... *I woke up this morning*
> *And got myself a beer ...*"

The Hot Heads tile the smoky air with hard slabs of industrial strength blues, and Hermann's seems a little smaller than usual. I find Abe sitting alone at a table in the shadows.

So you're just sitting here by yourself?

Abe gets up, we hug, and we both sit down. On the table, there's an empty coffee cup, half a dozen crushed creamer containers and an ashtray with two butts.

Abe says how was the free beer?

I came to get you first.

The smiling waitress comes by with a coffee pot, but Abe waves it away and orders a pint of pale ale. I order a glass of stout and, when it comes, drink it in two gulps. The music on stage is pretty good, all the nervous kids get in their licks, but I'm restless just sitting here in Hermann's where everybody just sits tonight at the tables. It seems to me that there are tables everywhere, tables between me and moving around, tables between me and other people. I don't like it, just sitting here at a table. I'm a single guy on a blues night, and I want to move around.

Abe is already drinking another pale ale though, so we hunker down and listen to the blues. Abe likes to lean up on his chair with his hand on his chin and his elbow on his knee and look closely at the fingerings of the jammers on their electric guitars.

> *". . . So let it roll, baby, roll,*
> *Let it roll all night long . . ."*

I say I've had enough. I'm going down to Bart's to look at women and move around and try to talk to them.

Abe says I'm coming, too.

We get up from the table, and it was like I was tied to my chair. We don't get to Bart's fast enough for me.

The place is packed, but they're still giving away free beer tickets at the door. You have to kind of nudge yourself around, lean in close to the women, smile, be cool, hello to everyone who smiles back, and you take it from there.

Abe wants a bottle of beer because of the crowd, but I get a pint of pale ale and start drinking. And moving around. I'm a single guy, a celibate sensualist, on a blues night, and I'm crazy to spend time with women.

Just be cool.

Be friendly.

Keep moving around.

The blues is a happy music that comes from a deep spot of lonesome pain in the naked human body. Upbeat, lowdown and brokenhearted, the blues make you smile and laugh and dance with a wild crowd of crazy people. When blues musicians reach down to that deep spot together, they make a basic, simple, electric music that throbs and howls with lonely, naked recognitions, and there's nothing but you have got to boogie.

I drift onto the dance floor where people are jumping up and down, begging the saxophone player to hit the roof, and when he does, the roof blows off and, boom boom bang, we are all one with the blues jam. We are the citizens of the evening's community.

> "... *You know I'm here,*
> *Everybody knows I'm here* ..."

On a stool at the bar, crossing her legs, is Tofu, a young woman who always says hello and talks to me at the jams. I like to move, I like to be cool, and I move in right beside her, and we begin to chat and laugh and flirt. Abe comes over. I introduce him to Tofu, but she sees a girlfriend across the room, and Abe and I are left with each other.

What we both need is another beer, so we go around the bar the way we came in and stand in line for service. I say hello to a couple of young and pretty women. One of them is Willamena, the waitress who was playing bumper hip with me last Saturday. The other woman is Starr, a big, happy gal who works down at Steamers in the kitchen. Hey, these are two young women, talking to a couple of young bucks, and I'm an old guy and have to be cool. I get a mug of beer and hang around, listening to the music.

> "... *Everybody knows I'm here,*
> *I'm the hoochie coochie man ...*"

Every once in a while someone is touching me from behind, touching my left hand, my forearm, my lower back. The touch is light, but it is warm, too, very warm and, on my next exhalation of breath, I shudder. The laser-hot tip of someone's finger is burning a small hole through my cotton shirt just above a kidney. It is painful and so delicious that I turn around and catch Willamena's hands gesturing broadly as she tells a funny story to the young bucks who respond like puppets on string.

I move in a step closer to catch her eye, and pretty soon her story is told, and she's talking to me. I introduce her to Abe.

Willamena is stunned, blurts out she had no idea I was old enough to have a son this old.

Abe laughs and says how old do you think I am?

Willamena says twenty-four.

Abe laughs again. That's how old I am alright.

I mumble something stupid like I have to tell the truth. What am I talking about?

Willamena says I would never have guessed you were old enough to be a father.

She laughs.

I mean a father of a guy that big.

We both look at Abe.

Yeah, he'd be hard to hide.

Willamena takes my hand in hers and squeezes. What's going on here? This good-looking, friendly young woman is obviously attracted to me, but she must be the same age as Abe. I don't have any cool at all now, I'm awkward as hell. Willamena is awkward, too.

She says excuse me.

She ducks under the counter where we've been standing, and she's gone.

> "... *If I done somebody wrong,*
> *Have mercy on me, please* ..."

Abe and I find a place to sit down in front of the tiny stage and take in the rest of the jam without protection. And then, it's good night.

Good night.

Good night.

Everybody in the bar is heading for the door, and we put on our coats and take our last dregs drink. It's a happy crowd, a whooping, chatty bunch, but I'm suddenly very blue.

Good night.

I always get the blues when the house band drummer puts away his sticks. I'm moping in the middle of the happy crowd, looking for a hole to open up so I can slip out of here and, wow, Willamena is beside me, beaming with drunken joy.

She says I'm going to Big Bad John's. Come and have a drink with me.

I say sure.

She says great.

And she's gone.

I find Abe waiting for me outside on the sidewalk.

He says what's up, Pops?

I don't know, but there's this woman—

He says Willy.

Yeah, Willamena.

He says she seemed to like you a lot as far as I could tell. She sure wasn't interested in me.

So, you don't think I'm making this up?

Abe laughs.

He says if your ex saw you with a woman like Willy, she'd flip.

Really? You think so?

Abe says I know so.

Well, Willamena wants me to meet her at Big Bad John's for a drink. You want to go up there?

Abe says well, I guess you better anyway.

We walk up the street to Big Bad John's.

At the door, Abe says follow me.

He goes in. I take another breath and exhale. It's nippy tonight.

I open the door and step into the bright lights of the noisy bar, and Willamena is screaming my name. She's sitting at a table with Starr and half a dozen young drunken male admirers. Willamena climbs over a guy sitting beside her, steps on the table and jumps.

She says catch me.

I catch her in my arms and put her down.

Willamena laughs.

She says I want to buy you a drink.

You're going to buy me a drink?

She says you and your son. I'm going to buy you both a drink.

Okay.

Abe and I order drinks, and the three of us are standing around.

I say so, where you from?

She says Campbell River.

Wow. I lived in Campbell River for ten years. We grew up there.

Abe says I grew up there.

Right. That's what I meant.

Abe and Willamena talk about growing up there, but they don't make any connections with mutual friends or anything. I'm perplexed, and must look so to Willamena.

She says I'm thirty-five years old.

You're thirty-five?

She says yes.

That's great. That's just great.

Willamena laughs. She takes me by the hand and leads me back to her table where Starr is keeping their many admirers in line. I sit down close beside Willamena, and Abe squeezes in beside me. Everybody's laughing and smoking, eating peanuts and drinking beer.

Willamena and I are deep into conversation about this and that, something about an ex-husband. Guess I'm getting drunk, losing details of narrative, logic, grammar . . . what did you say?

The whole scene blurs and begins to turn.

I have my arm around Willamena, and then I have my hand on her thigh. Careful. I'm just a little hot, and suddenly Willamena is very hot.

I say you're warm.

She says I'm always warm. I hope that's okay.

That's okay.

I laugh.

I like warm women.

I get a strong smell of her, and it drives me mad.

You smell wonderful.

Abe leans across the table and asks Willamena something about her ex-husband. She starts to answer the question, but I'm looking at her, looking into her eyes.

She says excuse me.

She gets up and goes to sit with a woman at a table across the room.

Abe says I don't think you should have left your hand on her thigh.

Well, I don't think you should have brought up the ex-husband again.

Starr surveys the table.

She says all you guys want to sleep with Willy tonight. But I'm the only one who gets to go home with her. I'm the only one who's going to sleep in the same room.

Everybody says yeah, yeah.

Starr says let me tell you another thing. All you guys want to play with my pectorals.

The guys howl.

Starr says all you guys want to bite my pectorals. But I'm the one playing with them, and I'm the one who's going to bite them.

Starr bites her tits. We are all impressed with her extraordinary flexibility and give Starr a vigorous round of applause.

One of the guys says give it to me, baby, give it to me.

Starr picks up a half pitcher of beer and pours it over his head. The young man jumps to his feet and performs an Irish jig. People are throwing peanuts and beer.

Abe decides he's had enough. He finishes his beer, says good night and heads for the exit.

I order another beer.

The room spins.

It's closing time, and the next thing I remember is being out on the street, trying to teach myself how to stand up without falling down. It's as hard as going to school.

Willamena and Starr are getting into a taxi. Their young, drunken admirers have followed them into the street, and one guy tries to get into the taxi, but Starr closes the door on his foot. The taxi drives away, and we're all left behind.

A guy runs after the taxi.

He is crying come back, come back, Willy, Willy, Willy—

A young woman follows him, grabbing his sleeve.

She says come here, baby, come here, baby, I know you're in love, but she's gone, come here, baby.

I turn and stumble ten blocks home. The electricity of the evening clings to me like a strong stink on my fingers. She didn't even say good night.

The Back Door Man

THREE NIGHTS GO BY without live blues. I want to move again, to jump up and down, to talk to some women. I put on a clean shirt, bundle up against the January cold and walk downtown on a Saturday night. There's lots of people on the streets, and live music pours out of all the clubs.

I walk into James Bay via Douglas to Avalon and down to the JBI. I get up to the door but stop and stand outside, looking in. On stage, The Harpoons are tuning guitars before their final set, and I can see people moving around, sitting at tables, standing at counters.

I can't go in. Walking in front of the band and everybody, I just can't, so I walk around the hotel through the parking lot into the back alley. I stand around for a while, then I walk in through the back door of the bar.

There's a whole bunch of happy people at a counter just inside the door, and Willy is their waitress. I duck into the men's can and look at myself in the mirror.

Finally, I return to the bar and stand behind everybody. I can't even see the band. Willy walks by with her tray, and she doesn't see me. She turns and walks by again. It's as if I don't even exist.

I'm thinking I said or did something wrong the other night. Either that, or she's embarrassed about her own actions and now wants to pretend nothing ever happened between us. I'm nothing to her. Never was. She was drunk. I was drunk. If she feels anything for me, it's total regret.

I fade to the back of the bar, putting on my coat and hat. Without saying good night to anyone, I turn on the happy crowd and go out the back door just as the band kicks in at full throttle.

Four or Five Pints of Beer

FOLLOWING THE BLUES SCENE makes rigorous physical demands on the body. It's pretty easy to drink four or five pints of beer at an afternoon jam, and it's still afternoon. Most people in the bar are smokers, too, and being an ex-smoker, I don't seem to mind a little poisonous air.

None of this is good for my health. To compensate, I have to workout all the time. I walk an average of ten miles a day. I lift weights in a gym three times a week. I do my stretches every morning. I do 200 sit-ups a day. I maintain a low-fat, high-fibre diet. I drink eight glasses of water a day. I eat fresh fruit and veg.

A blues fanatic is like a boxer. I have to try to stay in shape because I risk getting beat up every night. And the harder, the meaner the blues, the more the lonesomeness grows like a gnawing hunger in the pit of my stomach. The only way I can move around and try to talk to women is to be constantly in training.

Saturday afternoon, I got myself together, ironed a shirt, rolled a

joint, brushed my teeth, combed my two hairs and took off walking across town at a brisk pace to catch, yeah, the Saturday afternoon blues jam, which is the biggest need in my life right now.

In the bar, I find a spot in the centre of the room at a stand-up table, leaning back with thumbs in pockets Neal Cassidy-style. There's a lot of women here today, and more women keep coming in through the door, and they all walk right by me, brush up against me, lean in close, whispering in my ear: Hello, how are you?

Fine, fine, how are you?
Here's Willy handing me a glass of dark beer.
I say is everything okay?
She says always a little frantic when I first come to work.
She's not looking at me.
No, is everything okay between us?
She says did I give you the wrong change?
You're not upset with me about anything, are you?
Finally, she looks at me.
She says no.
She drags it out, a long no, and she turns with her tray and walks away in a hurry. She's laughing and smiling.
Good.
I know she hears me because she winks and looks right at me for a moment before she's gone. I turn around, and Brenda, pretty woman, is standing beside me.
She says you look happy.
Let's dance.
Brenda and I grab hold of each other and bolt for the dance floor.

Brenda says the blues are orgasmic.

Wow.

Although I wander broken-hearted and hopeless for purpose, today I have made a connection with the life of the blues and its women. This is why I work so hard to stay in shape. This is what I live for.

Raining Outside

GREY SKY AND BLUE FUNKY MIND. It's raining outside. Inside, nerve ends flare, popping sparks of electricity like severed cables of a power line down across a road, flailing out of control. Out of simple concern, I have to ask myself: Am I losing it?

Abe left town without leaving a note or phone message. I know he's young and might have been hungover. In my early 20s, I did much more than that to my pop, but the fact that Abe's gone puts some blues on the invention of the evening past, which I recall as a vigorous journey from bar to bar and blues band to blues band.

Two phone calls, one each from ex-wife and ex-girlfriend, do not help. Both women still want to control me, neither wants to give me a hug. Without a lover, which way do I turn? The past is a whole junkyard of broken wheels, and the future is scary and dim out along the darkening edges of the rain where I go looking for the light, the music and the women.

> "... *How long, baby, how long*
> *Has that evening train been gone* ..."

Out walking on a Saturday afternoon in the rain, and I'm punching the wet air with my fists. I sing out loud, laughing and dancing on the sidewalk, because I know, although empty and blue, chances of surviving one more night are good.

It's about four o'clock at the JBI, too late to get drunk in the afternoon, and I order a pint of dark beer with great confidence. The bar is packed with blues lovers, and everyone but me is smoking a cigarette. There's grey waves of smoke rolling through the low-ceilinged room, coming at me like early morning shit out of a pulp mill. I'm simultaneously smoking a hundred cigarettes, and I go outside to catch my breath with fresh air.

You can see the Legislature Buildings from here. There's Captain Vancouver without an umbrella, standing at the top of the dome. Or is it Captain Cook?

The door opens, and Brenda, pretty woman, steps out with a friend of hers, a forget-his-name guy that she's been playing pool with inside.

She says hi.

The three of us smoke a joint in the early February rainy chill.

I say today's my mom's birthday.

Forget-his-name says how old's your mom?

She's dead.

Brenda says brrr, I'm going back in.

I hang around for the rest of the jam, not really talking to anyone. Brenda and her guy are playing pool. The music gets louder and louder, and repetitive as if all the musicians are stuck on one 12-bar loop of mediocrity. I sit in drifting tobacco smoke, drinking three, four, six, seven glasses of beer. I stop counting and order a chicken burger.

The jam is over. The bar begins to empty, but I'm too stoned and too drunk and too fat to move. I switch to drinking black coffee. The bar begins to fill up again. Eight o'clock, and a band is setting up on stage.

A young guy asks do you mind if we?

He and a young woman shrug their shoulders on cue.

I say no, no.

A dozen twenty-somethings pull up chairs to my table, and I'm one of the gang.

The young guy says I'm Daniel.

Pleased to meet you.

The young woman says Bet.

Bet? As in Betty?

Daniel says naw, you bet your life.

Oh, like poker.

Bet says choose your poison, Charlie.

The band on stage kicks into gear.

> "... I got my mojo working,
> I got my mojo working ..."

Me and my dozen new-found friends leap to our feet and begin to dance, jumping up and down until after midnight, and I'm still on my feet for the standing ovation. A soft body bumps me from behind. It's a married woman I know who seems to bump into me from time to time. Where the hell is her husband?

She says I'm going down to catch the last set at Steamers. Why don't you come down, too?

Good idea.

She winks. She pinches me.
Hey.
She's gone.
Everybody is drinking up and hugging everybody.
Good night.
Good night.
Back in the far corner of the bar, I see Willamena Passetti hugging and kissing some young goof. Where'd she pick him up? A schoolyard?
Good night.
I burst out the door and stumble alone into the shivering, teeth-chattering rain. I can't get to Steamers fast enough. That pinch hurt.

If I Done Somebody Wrong

FRIDAY NIGHT, I STAND at the doors of The Glad Tidings Church on Quadra Street and look in. The gospel singers The Blind Boys of Alabama are whooping it up in front of five hundred people. An electrifying musical union of flesh and spirit, they wail, shout, cry and jump for Jesus. Shouting is the mother of the blues. Wild, wild, wild Clarence Fountain can jump as high as heaven, holding a note to the end of time. This blind old man with ten gold rings on his ten fingers is a human trinity of flesh, art and belief. Five hundred men, women and children jump with Clarence, jump up and down and howl with joy. Howling with joy is an antidote to doubt, to pain, to the terror of existence. Five hundred, all but one, howling, whooping and jumping.

> "... *Listen, listen now,*
> *Listen to the lambs all cry* ..."

Later, I'm sitting all alone in Hermann's, listening to the Hot Heads. Slim Harris wields his slide guitar like a laser. The young kids at the next table hoot and howl, beating the tabletop with their fists. But it's all a strange, buzzing fatigue in my ears, a buzzing like electrical, alien insects chewing and tearing away my consciousness. I am so tired, so very, very tired, that I can't fight against the drifting lonesomeness.

Lord, have mercy on me.

I talk out loud, and the young kids look at me funny.

Almost Stayed Home Blues

WITHOUT PURPOSE, WITHOUT PROTECTION, I lie on the floor and pretend my fragile being is a satellite drifting swiftly into infinity. Takes all I can do to sleep all day and chase the blues all night. There's some doubt and despair in this selfish, self-inflicted life without purpose, but as long as the gold card is good, I don't foresee a change of plans.

Hours go by. A few minutes anyway. I get up, put on my coat, go down to the street and don't stop walking until I slide into Swans on a Monday night when the jump blues band Barrelhouse is blowing at full throttle. Al Pease wails on his sax, and Clark Brendon, smug and cool on standup bass, lets it all hang out.

People jump up from the tables and dance around their chairs. Everybody is jumping up and down. I drum my palms on the bar top. A pretty blonde laughs at me. I laugh back.

She says you want to dance?

Yeah.

We jump up and down and bump and rub up against each other, trading sweat and laughter. She hoots. I hoot. She hollers, and I holler. We hoot and whistle. I'm cool, and I'm hot. The celibate sensualist never grabs and never takes. I dance along the razor's edge of desire and intimacy. Playing with fire.

The band shuts it down, and the bar explodes. The pretty blonde and I hug each other, step back and laugh.

She says Friday.

Friday?

She says that's my name.

Oh.

She says do you want to come home with me?

I don't know.

She says I just moved here from Nelson. I've got some pot.

Okay.

She says you must be a happy person.

No, I'm sad and lonely.

She says oh, yeah.

We drift across downtown, wandering down Douglas, cutting behind the bus station to cross the street to the museum. Totems behind glass carve five hundred years of rain. Raven transforms into Bear into Salmon into Eagle. Wild Man. Wild Woman. Thunderbird. A fountain bubbles pastel neon. We wait for a car to go by before crossing another street. Friday and I look at each other and laugh.

We haven't said a word since the bar.

Friday says magic.

The car, pulled by light into eternity, finally passes, and we cross the street into James Bay. A creaky staircase takes us up above a bicycle shop into a funky hallway saturated with a scratchy John Coltrane solo. Friday knocks once on an apartment door and goes right on in.

She says come on.

> "... *A love supreme,*
> *A love supreme ...*"

I follow Friday through the door, and sitting cross-legged on the living room floor are Bet and Daniel. Daniel is rolling a joint. In front of him is a bag of weed big as a head of lettuce.

Bet says oh, hi, you, so, you, like, met my sister.

The four of us sit cross-legged on the floor and share counterclockwise a couple of joints. Cough. John Coltrane rules.

How did you get the name Friday?

She says my parents were a couple of hippies.

I was a hippie.

She says no kidding.

All four of us think that's pretty funny, and we burst into laughter, rich and fat and juicy, of the moment, and it goes around the small circle like four little kids sharing a watermelon on a summer's day out of time.

Bet picks up a harp and begins to blow. Daniel strums a guitar and sings a lonely blues song about a woman who went away and won't be coming back. Friday bounces and moves around. She leans on me and squeezes against me, and it feels good. I'm hot. But I'm cool. I'm hot, and I'm on my feet.

Bet says oh, you're not going.

Yeah. Good night.

Good night.
Good night.
Good night.
I'm so cool. Through the cold, dark night, I walk home with my hard-on.

Sex in the 90s

THE FEBRUARY PLUM BLOSSOMS foam down Wharf Street to the foot of Bastion Square. The full moon is a plum blossom, too. A ragged busker sweetens the evening more.

> "... *Ain't got no cigarettes,*
> *King of the road ...*"

I skip up the steps to Harpo's, pull out my ticket for Junior Wells and squeeze my way inside to a thick and smoky noisy mob of down and dirty blues fans. I buy a bottle of beer and, looking for a spot to hang out, end up politely plowing my way to the end of the bandstand. The techys are running sound checks.

A cheer goes up through the bar. Five or six guys break for the stage. Is that the band? There's a lot of electronic chaos, the crowd milling and bumping, the nerve ends bubbling like the water does before the salmon bite. Is that Junior? The stage lights come up on seven or eight guys picking up instruments. The drummer picks up his sticks. These guys are black, white, yellow, brown, a rainbow of people who make blues, and there's a roar of delight from the crowd when the trombone comes up to the mic and says hello, Victoria.

Before anyone can take a breath, there's a wall of Chicago blues in the room, and everybody begins to jump up and down. I'm jumping up and down, wildly dancing in the ocean of sound. The drummer is tock tock tock boom, and the bass player is digging himself a basement. There's a tinkling keyboard, a rhythm guitar, a lead guitar, a trumpet, a sax, and the trombone man who blares a solo of sexy, brassy blues.

Ladies and gentlemen, Junior Wells.

And there's Junior, all smiles and glitter, in his rings and his bowler and his immaculate electric-blue three-piece suit and tie. He's hot. He's jumping up and down. He pulls out his harp and begins to blow. One, two, three beautiful notes, and then he stops. What? He wants to break our hearts?

Junior says hey, hey.
We say hey, hey.
Junior says ho, ho.
We say ho, ho.
Junior says howdy, doody doody.
We say howdy, doody doody.
Junior says do you want the blues?
We say yeah.
Junior says what did you say?
We say yeah.
Junior says did you say blues?

Yeah.

Junior says that's what I got.

He blows his harp, and the band behind explodes into walls and waves of electric blues, and everybody in Harpo's jumps and bumps and rocks. Junior bumps and rocks. He jumps down into the crowd and boogies across the dance floor.

Junior is a pied piper on the blues harp. Everybody jumps in line behind him for a snakedance. We hop forward, hop back and hop hop hop, following Junior Wells all around the bar. The music is never going to stop, and then Junior dashes up the stairs to his dressing room and disappears. Boom boom crash.

The trombone says we'll be right back.

Outside, I'm leaning on the rail of the porch to Harpo's, looking out at rushing sky and sea, red and green lights in the inner harbour. I'm happy with blues and beer. I'm pretty simple, and I'm thinking I really love this town. I love the foaming streets, the plum blossoms, the neon. I love Junior Wells. I love being alive tonight. I love every goddamn healthy heartbeat, every blues moment. I love the blues.

People are looking at me. The echo of my voice ricochets off the buildings across the square. I've been shouting, but I don't care.

I love the blues.

People are laughing now. Some of them yell I love the blues, and it's one big hooting and hollering time on the Harpo's porch. Somebody opens the door to the club, and live blues pour out.

The crowd hangs around the edges of the dance floor, edgy and jumpy like pioneers before the start of a landrush. Whoa, Junior Wells is back on stage, and the band takes off.

> "... *Babe, you got to help me,*
> *I can't do it all by myself ...*"

I go out on the dance floor with everybody else and start jumping and moving and bumping. It's one o'clock in the morning, and nobody has a partner. Everybody is dancing with the band. I'm dancing with three different women all at once. This is live, electric, real, as hot as it gets for the horny celibate. Junior Wells is wailing, moaning, begging, humping, blowing his harp, and I'm hallucinating that the woman who keeps bumping me with her bum, this woman who is tall and round and happy in the delicious moment, is a woman I met on a bus between Saint Louis, Missouri, and Memphis, Tennessee, twenty-five years ago. We shared a ham sandwich and a mutual grope, and here she is all of a sudden again now. I almost come.

Junior dances up to the dressing room, goes in and closes the door. The band bangs out one last note, and the drummer puts away his sticks. The lights come up. The three women slip away, gone forever.

Oh, I have the blues, but I'm happy, too, and I'm yelling. Everybody is yelling. We howl. We beg. We howl and beg some more. And, hey, there's mercy in the world after all because here comes the band, walking back on stage and picking up their instruments. The drummer picks up his sticks, and they're all flying again. The dressing room door opens, and Junior Wells sticks out his head and sings.

> "... *See the lady with the diamond ring,*
> *She knows how to shake that thing ...*"

I dance alone in the middle of the dance floor. Jumping up and down. And here's that woman again, bumping into me and, okay, I begin to bump her, too, and, oh, I like this, I like, I love the blues, I love the blues, and yes, this time I do come in my pants. Boom boom bang.

Cup of Coffee Blues

I HANG OUT ALONE on a stool at the bar in Hermann's. The stage is bare. The coffee is awful but, hey, the celibate sensualist can always have his cake and eat it, too. Boom boom bang.

Why so smug?

It's Brenda, pretty woman, climbing up on the stool beside me, and Brenda is talking, words pouring out of her mouth like water from an open tap. Talking about her search for a new apartment. Talking about her two jobs and the job she got fired from. Talking about her sister, about the incredible jerk her sister married. Talking about how most men in general are jerks, present company an exception of course.

Oh?

I can't keep up with all the details, but she doesn't seem to care. I feel a little pinched-in and wouldn't mind finding a way out of here. We're not a couple. I'm not her date. I came down here for the bad coffee and bare stage, not companionship. I'm beyond relationships.

Dead air.

Brenda says what did you say?
I think I'm out of here.
Brenda says where are you going?
Down to Bart's.
Brenda says let's go.
She jumps down from her stool and starts putting on her coat.
I want to finish first.
Brenda says awful coffee.
I don't know how to not go with her down to Bart's without a hassle and bad feelings. No, I don't want that. I'd rather be uncomfortable. I drink the burned coffee and put on my coat.
Let's go.
Brenda casually takes my arm as we walk down the street.
She says you're different than other guys.
Oh, yeah?
She says yeah, you don't mind a woman who talks.
At Bart's, we run into Old Bob Texas and his girlfriend Tammy. Bob always says even when I was a young boy, they called me Old Bob. Not my favourite person, but Brenda knows Tammy, and they start talking. There's a third woman, too.
I say hi, how's it going?
She says better if we had some pot.
I wouldn't know about that.
She says liar.
Old Bob introduces me to Lana.
Lana says I'm trying to get into cop school.
Is it hard?
She says, oh, yeah, but I've got a record.
Oh.

She says for drugs.
So, are you a cop?
Lana picks up a menu.
She says how are the oysters?
Lana studies the menu. Old Bob is talking to Brenda and Tammy. I tap him on the shoulder.
Is she a cop?
Old Bob shrugs.
I shrug.
Lana says how can they sell oysters in here when they're out of season?
That's not true.
She says what do you know?
Ask the bartender.
She says he works here.
I don't think he's pushing tainted oysters.
She says what is he pushing?
Brenda taps me on the shoulder.
She says I'm ready to go.
Me, too.
Lana says I'm talking to you.
I nod my head. I'm thinking one woman on the street is better than two women in the bar. I put on my coat. I look Brenda in the eye.
Let's go.
Lana says when will I see you again?
I'll be around.
She says tomorrow night?
Maybe.

She says I'll be here tomorrow night.
Good night.
Brenda and I walk up Douglas to Fort, then east on Fort past Cook, all the way Brenda is talking about the incredible jerk who married her sister, and by the time we get to her apartment building, I hate the guy.
We hug.
Good night.
Brenda says you want to come up?
Not tonight, thanks.
Brenda says what's the problem?
What?
Brenda climbs the steps to her front door.
At the top, she turns and says have a good life, Charlie.
You think I got a problem?
Brenda goes through the door and, click, closes it quickly but quietly. Beyond relationships, I turn and walk ten blocks home. Except for the siren crying down Cook Street, I don't hear another word.

The Thing To Do

LAST NIGHT THE THING TO DO is to go down to Harpo's for John Hammond and The Duke Robillard Band, so here I am at the door, 9:30, and all I hear from inside is canned pop pap muzak.

What's going on?

The doorman says John Hammond is coming on in an hour.

An hour?

The doorman shrugs. People push their way around me through the door. I give in and join the stream. Inside, there's hardly room to move, and I don't see anyone I know.

I hear someone calling my name, and I see Bet and Daniel and Friday at a table a few feet away from the dance floor. For some reason, Bet and Daniel are having an intense conversation about Tristan Tzara. Was it the furry spoon or the urinal on a pedestal that flushed modernism down the toilet?

I have no opinion about crap like that.

Someone kicks me under the table.

When I hear the word "Tzara," I reach for my shin guard.
Bet says will you shut up?
Don't kick people.
I sense the conversation is not going well. I turn to Daniel.
I say so, did you listen to that tape I loaned you?
Bet says what tape?
"Everybody Digs Bill Evans".
Daniel says I'm going to listen to it tonight, after.
Bet says what does Bill Evans have to do with German expressionism after World War I?
I shake my head. Unless I agree with every bit of pretentious misinformation spilling out of Bet's pretty head, she'll think I'm picking on her.
Sorry, but I left my library book at home.
Maybe I am picking on her.
Bet and Daniel wrap around one another and begin to french kiss. Friday sucks on a cigarette.
So, how's your furry spoon tonight?
Friday laughs.
She says oh, I'm not much into anything right now, and I really, really dig it.
Who are these people?
I take my beer and drift into the pressing crowd. On stage, one of the bouncers unfolds a single metal chair, and a roady places an acoustic guitar on the seat. The crowd cheers. A big man with a full head of silvery blonde hair picks up the guitar and sits down. There's a squeal of feedback.
The big man says good evening, Victoria. My name is John Hammond.

When we finally quiet down, John Hammond delivers an hour of unplugged, down home, drugstore country blues.

> "... *Woke up this morning,*
> *Looking around for my shoes* ..."

I first saw John Hammond live thirty years ago at a club in Boston. He was just a kid then, and so was I. But the years pass by, both of us are now guys a little gone to seed and purposelessness, and Hammond has earned an authenticity through his art that is heartbreakingly real. When he sings his baby left him and he'd do anything for her return, I believe it. And the two hundred people pressing up against him tonight believe it, too. Hammond cries the blues.

> "... *Come on in my kitchen,*
> *It's going to be raining outside* ..."

John Hammond says I'm going take a break.
Alright.
Someone pinches me.
Hey.
Old Bob Texas steps out of the crowd. He squeezes his index finger against his thumb as if to squish a bug, and laughs.
What the fuck you doing?
Old Bob says you should connect with Tammy.
What?
Old Bob says outside, you know.
I walk down the front steps of Harpo's into the square. Cold and

clear. Fresh air feels good like a washcloth. I wander down a narrow alley of cobbled stone, leading to a dumpster behind a restaurant where the air is dense with the stench of rotten meat. Two more steps, and it's the harsh sweetness of Lasqueti Island bud.

Tammy hands me a hot little pipe of green smoke. I take a big toke, bend over, coughing so hard that stars fall like rain in my eyes.

Thanks.

Tammy lights the pipe again. I take another toke, and the euphoria of the burning weed saturates my brain.

Tammy giggles. She says lucky you found me.

I ran into Bob.

She says bastard pinched me. Look.

Her forearm has a mark on it like a red grape.

You need some ice.

Tammy says I need a guy who's nice.

Lots of those around.

Tammy says you think so?

Tammy drops her right arm and, in a backhoe motion, brings her open hand up into the crotch of my pants. She squeezes my soft cock and balls as if inspecting the ripeness of an avocado in a market. She puts her left hand behind my neck and buries her tongue into the roof of my mouth. Thusly trussed, I gasp.

And step away from her grasp.

Tammy says you don't like me.

I like you.

I laugh.

Tammy says you think I'm funny?

Despite the cold air, bubbles of sweat spread across my forehead. Loudly, almost shouting, I say I think I'm funny, okay?

Tammy says Bob's an asshole.
I know.
Tammy says we don't even live together.
Good for you.
Tammy says you gay, or what?
I'm celibate.
Tammy says celibate?
You're the first person I've ever told, but yeah.
Tammy says you don't even beat off?
Hey, that's between me and my right hand.
Tammy and I both laugh.
Tammy says I'm cold.
Well, let's go back in.

Tammy holds out her hand, and I take it. We walk down the alley, across the square, up the steps to Harpo's, and all the way we're holding hands.

Inside the club, Duke Robillard has been playing for some time. The crowd is so thick we can hardly move. Tammy drifts away, and the sudden anonymity in the loud, dark, thick frenzy gives me an instant erection. I become one with the swelling beast of dance, anonymous strangers combining into one electric body of bumping and jumping up and down. The warm, soft bump of breasts, like red mango, grazes arms and shoulders. Let's enjoy the passage of the one eternal moment. Enjoy life.

Boom boom boom bang crack. Duke Robillard brings down an electric silence within which one foreboding mortal note quivers in the air above the immobile dancers. My ears are beehives. I am soaked in a downpour of my own sour sweat. The club is hot and stinks like sweetly-rotten sex. What a sewer of fun.

Duke Robillard says get John Hammond back up here.

John Hammond climbs the two steps to the stage, goes to the mic and begins to cry.

> "... If you're going cheat on me,
> Don't cheat on me unkind ..."

I dance alone, and that's a funny thing to say in a room so crowded I can hardly take a step without bumping into somebody's soft flesh and sharp stink. A bubble of brokenhearted pain begins to expand beneath my chest between my lungs and my ribcage. The skin of the bubble must be made of lead. It is so heavy and almost, almost hurts too much.

> "... When you done cheating on me,
> Please, please, please find the time ..."

Despite the boom boom of the roaring room, I think I can hear the sinewy ligaments that hold my ribcage together begin to snap. And now, as if a dam has burst, my cheeks, my face, my lips, my chin drips with a shower of saltwater so hot it feels like each drop must leave a little white welt of blister on my skin. I'm dancing and crying.

> "... Crawl back into my bed, baby,
> And love me kind ..."

I want to sit down somewhere. Bet throws her arms around me and gives me a big hug.

She says are you alright?
I've been crying like an idiot.
She says have you seen Daniel?
No.
She says we're having a fight. I better go look for him.
Bet is gone, and now Friday falls into my arms.
Friday says I want to dance.
We dance. We try to dance. Friday wants her drink, and I dance alone. The music never stops.
And then, it stops.
John Hammond says good night, Victoria.
The club erupts into hoots, hollers, whistles and screaming. We pick up empty beer bottles and bang their glass bottoms on tabletops. The lights come up. Duke Robillard and John Hammond are gone. The drummer and his sticks are gone, too. The music is over and ain't coming back, but nobody gets ready to go home yet. Instead, we bang and bang and bang the bottles because it seems to be the thing to do.

Here Am I

HERE AM I AT A TABLE with a pint, sitting beside Abe in Swans on a Monday night when Barrelhouse is playing. There's a trombone from Toronto sitting in, and the band is extra hot. Everybody claps and whoops, talking back to the band. Alright.

Dave Harris sings a sad blues about a woman who goes away and finds another man, and I am suddenly very sad. A chasm appears to open up between me and everybody else, and I plunge downward, darkly inside myself. I reach out and take Abe's left hand in my right hand and squeeze hard.

Abe says what's up, Pops?

Wow, I don't know. I'm having a little trouble breathing.

Abe says you okay?

Whew, just, just give me—

I try to stand up.

Abe says careful.

It's so goddamn smoky in here.

I'm having trouble standing up. Abe gets up and helps me. Whew, okay.

Abe says let's go outside.

Abe helps me walk toward the exit.

Charles Gates holds out a steady hand as I pass, making sure I don't impale myself on his drum kit. He laughs into the mic.
He says is there a doctor in the house?
I yell back is there a drummer?
Everybody laughs.
Abe and I snap through the exit to the street. I gulp at the night air like it's water.
Abe says you okay?
Oh, man, whew, yeah.
I lean against the brick wall of Swans. It feels strong enough to take all my weight, and I relax.
I'm sure glad I grabbed your hand when I did.
Abe says I'm glad, too.
Thanks.
Abe says any time, Pops.
I was sitting there listening to the band, and suddenly I was real sad.
Abe says sad about what?
Sad about everything, I guess, sad about last year, this year, next year, next week, fuck.
Abe says you have to get over it.
What?
Abe says I'm not saying anything.
Who?
Abe says I'm going back in.
Her?
Abe says excuse me.
Ah, come on, stay out here with me. Don't get uptight.
Abe says you're uptight.

I'm leaning against a goddamn building, how's that uptight?
Abe shakes his head.
This doesn't have anything to do with women.
Abe says forget it.
What am I saying? Of course, my whole life has had everything to do with women.
Abe says I found a new word.
A new word.
Abe says acedia.
What's that got to do with women?
Abe spells out the word.
What's it mean?
Abe says pathological spiritual apathy.
I laugh.
That's pretty heavy, and it's still only 10:30.
Abe says it also means sloth regarded as one of the seven deadly sins.
So you think what?
Abe says what do you think?
Thanks for the word. Acedia.
Abe says well?
What, what?
Abe says do you think that's me?
You?
Abe says what do you think?
That's ridiculous.
Abe says it is?
Yes.
Abe says in Greek, it means "without care."

Without care?
Abe says yeah.
That doesn't apply to you at all. You always take care of yourself real well.
Abe says well, it's something to think about.
Say, sorry about getting uptight.
Abe says forget it.
No, this is important—
Abe laughs.
What's so funny?
Abe says oh, you know, how women say guys never talk about this stuff.
Who's talking about women?
Abe laughs.
Okay, it's a theme.
Abe says so, how did the Jays do today?
I don't know. I was trying to say something—
Abe says guys only talk about sports.
Ernest Humingway pops through the exit. He's looking around for someone.
Ernest. Who won the ball game?
Ernest says so, you survived your panic attack?
What?
Ernest says or heart attack—
Wasn't a heart—
Ernest says not.
He laughs and says but you're okay?
Yeah, yeah.
Ernest lights a cigarette.

Abe says did you hear the score?
Ernest says you know, there's guys your age who just drop dead like that.
Like guys my age? You're my age.
Ernest says right.
He sucks on his cigarette.
Ernest says I'd quit smoking, but there's no way I'm giving up a vice.
You know, sometimes I feel—
Ernest says oh, we're sensitive tonight. Male bonding—
Fuck you, man.
Ernest says no, no, I apologize. What do you feel?
Forget it.
Abe says sometimes I feel like an uprooted tree.
Ernest laughs.
Abe says that's dumb.
Ernest says no, I can see it, the roots of the tree going every which way and no earth to stick them in.
Ernest laughs.
He says I'm going back in.
Ernest opens the exit door, and live blues pours out of the bar. We can hear a woman inside screaming with joy.
Abe says you okay?
He says I love you, Pops.
Love you, too.
Abe says after you.
He follows me into the dark, delicious throes of the swinging upbeat fray, bang bang boom.

The Saxophone Case

I SIT WITH A COFFEE in a booth by the window in a downtown café. The coffee is muddy and lukewarm, the porcelain cup is not clean. Saxophone jazz scratches out of a little plastic radio. The waitress and the cook have both disappeared. The window on Quadra Street is a bebop of hail, rain, sunshine and wind. Sharply-focussed women full of female purpose rush by.

I study my *VISA* statement and cannot believe my good fortune. I had it figured I'd be living on the streets in less than a month. I didn't have the credit to borrow enough to pay the minimum, a dead bust. But now, here's a five thousand dollar boost to my credit limit, and I'm back in business. I was beginning to fear I might have to look for a job, purpose, or meaning but, thank god, I can now abandon all that nonsense. Five thousand bucks. Again, I wallow in spiritual malaise and purposelessness. I can afford to be a bum until at least the end of summer.

I keep running into this word "anomie" that all the hip, young writers in Toronto are bandying about. I looked it up, and it means "lawless wild abandon." Yeah, in Toronto. Given a choice though, I'd still rather have the gold card.

A guy about seventy, my dad's age, slides into the booth across from me. He has a saxophone case.

He says how's the coffee?

Awful.

He says too bad.

Nobody seems to be working here today. Want me to get you a cup?

He says I don't drink coffee.

This is your lucky day.

He says every day is my lucky day.

So, you play?

He says I play bridge.

You just carry around a saxophone?

He says what makes you think it's a saxophone?

It's a saxophone case.

He says yes, it's a saxophone case.

Okay.

He says I played for forty years as a professional sideman and studio musician in Los Angeles. I toured with Stan Kenton. I recorded with Frank Sinatra, Tony Bennett, Ella.

Wow. Congratulations.

He says I've had two by-pass operations in five years and don't dare play. I'm terrified of my saxophone and never leave it out of my sight.

The old man laughs.

He says I had my first heart attack just minutes before a gig. I felt this flame go up my arm. I shook it off, went out and played for four hours. I had my best solo ever that night. The last note I hit held time and silence blowing pure.

    He says backstage, after the last set, I could barely make the phone call. An ambulance picked me up in front of the theatre and took me to the hospital where the doctor was already sharpening his knives.

    Lawless wild abandon.

    He says that's the way I played that night. Best solo ever.

Yes.

CURTAIN.

Playwright, poet, and spoken jazz artist, Charles Tidler is a Hoosier in Canada. The father of two sons, he makes his home in Victoria.